A Disaster Atlas

Dealing with the aftermath
of a terrorist attack,
in several forms.

by T H. Harbinger

Copyright © 2021 by Insights on Innovation, LLC

All rights reserved. This book or any portion thereof may not be reproduced or used in any manner whatsoever without the express written permission of the publisher except for the use of brief quotations in a book review.

Printed in the United States of America

First Printing, 2021

This work is a memoir. The places, dates, and incidents are authentic and based on records from various archives.

Please visit the author's website:
https://www.amazon.com/T-H.-Harbinger/e/B00JEVD256

ISBN: 9798507978953

Cover Photo: Middletown remembers 9.11 – The Round Table

Inside Photo: Rand McNally Pocked Road Atlas, ISBN 0-528-24484-1

A Disaster Atlas

Table of Contents

A Disaster Atlas

Foreword

"Remember the hours after Sept. 11 when we came together as one! It was the worst day we have ever seen, but it brought out the best in all of us." — John Kerry

Chapter 1 A Barn Fire

New Jersey
11 September 2001

A woman burst into our meeting shouting, "The Trade Center's been bombed!"

My colleague, Bharat Pant, the person assigned to learn all he could from me, blurts out, "Not again."

He jumps from his chair and motions for the rest of us to follow. Bharat runs to the east end of the hallway, where a large window offers a panoramic view of downtown New York City. He freezes solid as he glares out the window. As I catch up behind him, I immediately see. The North Tower of the World Trade Center, the one to our left, is spewing smoke near the building's top.

We watch in silence as black and white smoke steams out. By now, twenty people are standing behind Bharat and me. An image forms in my mind. One from my childhood.

It was a hot summer afternoon, and I was raking hay into swaths for baling the next day. I was driving our SC Case tractor pulling behind the two-wheeled eight-foot hay raking machine. As I turned toward the west end of the field a flash caught my eye. I looked to the south and saw our neighbor's, the Hoppie's, barn spewing smoke much like I now saw from the World Trade Center. I wanted to do something but couldn't figure out what to do. I couldn't drive the equipment through the marsh to that barn. I couldn't unhook the rake as it would fall to the ground, and I wouldn't be able to lift it to hook back up. I could stop and run to the fire, but what could I do once I got there. It would take me at least a half-hour to run that far through the marsh and jump how many barbed wire fences.

A thought comes and I whisper it, "That building is coming down."

My comment wakes Bharat from his daze. He turns to the group and motions for them to head back to their work. I walk with him slowly back to our meeting room.

As he walks, he mutters, "This situation brings back terrible memories for many of us."

I glance at him with a look of curiosity. He continues, "The same tower was attacked eight years ago, on February 26, 1993. Those of us who worked on our campus remember that day, as we will now always remember this day. A group of Middle Eastern terrorists detonated a truck full of explosives in the garage with the intent to send the North Tower crashing into the South Tower, bringing both towers down and killing tens of thousands of people. Fortunately, it failed to do so. Explosion experts determined the bomb used a plastic explosive called Semtex to trigger the massive explosion. Semtex was the only commercially produced component of the bomb. How the terrorists obtained Semtex was never disclosed. Still, many of us believe that material came from our chemical laboratory's basement, the building next to this one on our campus. One of our research chemists[1] has not been seen since the day before that bombing. Many have suspected us of negligence in not avoiding the disaster. We agonize wondering if we have responsibilities that go beyond our control."

Bharat stops at the open door of our meeting room. I walk past him, looking directly into his eyes, trying to convey a sense of understanding. However, the reason I'm in New York in the first place does not summon any sympathy with those that insisted I come.

They fall back into their chairs and attempt to continue the meeting. I stand at the head of the table, surrounded by Bharat's technical staff. This group will take over the leadership of the sensors and controls research and development for what is called 'the combined company.' We've been combined on paper for almost two years, but now is the deadline for real action. Bharat titled the meeting simply Integration. Business practices define these types of meetings as identifying the synergy of a merger or acquisition. More precisely, we are deciding which laboratories are closed and who will be laid-off.

I am the only person invited representing what we call 'the old Honeywell.' I try to re-start the discussion from where we were before the interruption. Of the four women and six men surrounding the table, no one is looking at me. They are making notes or helping themselves slowly to another sip of coffee. I'd been talking for about five minutes,

---

[1] I later learned that Abdul Rahman Yasin is considered the only participant in the 1993 World Trade Center bombing who was never caught.

uninterrupted, when the woman again flung open the door to shout, "The South Tower's been hit! It's not a bomb! It's airplanes!"

All ten attendees besides me gasp, with Bharat being the loudest. He sprints for the panoramic view once more. I trail the group to the window. The smoke emanating from the North Tower has subsided some but now smoke from the South Tower, a bit closer to the ground, bellows worse than the first.

Bharat stares and mumbles, "The 1993 attackers watched from New Jersey while waiting for the two towers to collapse."

Bharat's team members turn and push past me. Each shouts something as they pass.

"I have to get my kids."

"My kids are in school."

"My son went to the city today for a field trip."

"My brother works in the South Tower."

"I have to call my mother. She's not been feeling well."

"We're under attack!"

"Oh my god, I can't believe this is happening."

"I have to find my wife."

More people start coming out of all the offices. All are heading for the exits from this top floor of the headquarters building. It's not quite a panic rush, but almost.

Bharat stands next to me as we watch this exodus. There are some screams from the stairwells as it seems a few have tripped and fell. I hear the sounds of others grabbing them and helping them along amongst the panic sounds.

Bharat turns to me, "Our meeting is over. I have no idea when or how we might continue. Let's see if my assistant can help you. I think it best if you could leave. We all need to take care of our loved ones first."

I nod and follow him down two flights to his office. His assistant is about to leave the office. She shouts as Bharat approaches, "All the lines are busy. I can't get through to my daughter's school. I'm heading there now. The radio reports that all travel into and out of New York is banned, including airports."

She peels off. Bharat has already entered his office and collected a briefcase and car keys. He says as he passes, "I'm sorry, but it seems none of us can help you. You still have your hotel room, yes?"

And with that, he disappears into the stairwell. I look at my watch. It's 9:15 am.

Chapter 2 What Next?

Rand McNally Pocket Road Atlas page 25
11 September 2001

I have never felt this helpless before. I've been in several situations in the past but always maintained a level head. I was able to think when others could not. There was this time in high school when a group of us had been drinking. We decided to pack into a car and drive to another house. A few minutes into the trip, the vehicle veered off the gravel road into the ditch toward a tree. As others froze, I reached across the person in the middle and steered the car back onto the gravel from the passenger seat. The driver never took his foot off the accelerator pedal. I never thought much more about it. The middle seat passenger would recall the incident with great excitement over the next several outings, but I just let the story fade away.

I'm not able to come up with a thought of what to do next. I don't even want to try. I'm content in this zombie state. I start to walk, to at least follow others down the stairs and out the front door. I see black smoke filling the sky above the trees to the east. A thought does come into my mind: that building is coming down. I stand at the end of the walkway, watching people running to their cars only to drive a few feet and wait in a long line of jammed vehicles trying to exit the campus. This feeling of emptiness is new to me. There's a voice nagging inside of me to do something. But it seems so far away, so unimportant.

It's a beautiful blue sky, sunny morning. Birds are chirping in the trees as cars jam up in the parking lot. Somehow surrounded by this noise and activity, I don't see anything. Is it this action of trying to escape, this act of desperation, that has affected me? There's a stillness that surrounds me, yet I can see cars inching along, waiting their turn. They are the help that is on the way.

Maybe I should be help on the way for someone? That's what I usually was. Or at least I thought so. I had flown from Minneapolis two days ago for a meeting at our newly located Corporate Headquarters. It's a last-ditch effort to save my research group. Fourteen months ago, the company Allied Signal agreed to purchase the Minneapolis-based company where I worked. They wanted our customers, our products, our services, our funding, some of our buildings, and even our name. They just didn't want most of us. As I look back at the glass door on the headquarters building, Honeywell's name in solid red stands bold. Before they officially took ownership of the combined company, the new executive management replaced every sign and engraved door having the Allied Signal name and logo with equal signs and engraved doors displaying the Honeywell name. They had a plan.

The day the so-called merger was announced, only seven people were retained out of the thousand that worked in our headquarters building just south of downtown Minneapolis. My boss's boss was not one of them. Nine months ago, on the day of the official company merger, my boss lost his job. Now here I am on September 11, 2001, justifying my research group's benefit to the new company. Or at least I was before the World Trade Center attack. Now I stand outside the headquarters building, not knowing in which direction even to take another step. Yet there's mass panic all around me as people race to start their cars only to wait in a non-moving line. Some begin to honk their horns. Others open their side window and shout into the air. Do they know what to do? Are they going to help?

A woman comes running up behind me. She says, "Do you have a car?"

I look at her with a puzzled look as I slowly twist my head back and forth sideways.

She continues, "I saw you this morning in the hotel. Are you from Minneapolis?"

I slowly nod my head up and down.

"So am I. I was supposed to fly back this afternoon, but I can't get through to the airline to see about my flight. Someone told me the airports are being closed."

I look at her and stammer, "Do you know what is going on?"

She looks past me at the jammed cars in the parking lot and mumbles, "No."

She then collects herself and adds, "We aren't going to be any help to these people. I think it best if we somehow just get out of here."

I point, "I think that car is a rental. It has a National sticker on it."

"Come on," she says as she turns and heads back toward the building. "Let's see if we can find out who has it."

I follow her into the lobby as she heads for the stairs and is out of sight. There is a small group huddled around a radio behind the reception desk. I slowly shuffle in that direction, hoping to hear the broadcast. I stand in silence as we listen to a reporter shouting that airplanes have crashed into both the World Trade Center towers. It was thought to be a terrible accident, but now reporters are describing it as a terrorist attack. The city is locking down. The FAA has closed the airspace surrounding New York City to any air traffic. Fighter jets are being deployed to protect against any further attacks.

I wait for more than twenty minutes in the lobby. A few people leave, and others join the group listening to the broadcast. No words are spoken. Only gasps of grief and desperation are offered.

Suddenly, the reporter is shouting, "The tower is coming down. The tower is coming down. The South Tower is collapsing onto itself. I have to evacuate." And the broadcast goes dead.

After a minute, another voice comes across the radio. "It's estimated thousands have most likely been killed." It's 10 am.

The woman from outside comes running down the stairs carrying a suitcase and shouts, "I've got the car."

I say, "Whose is it?"

"Some guy upstairs. He's from upstate New York but has relatives nearby. He's going to stay with them till things settle down."

"Did you get the rental changed to your name?" I ask.

"We tried, but the lines are completely busy. When I saw one of the towers disappear, I decided it's time to leave. We'll straighten out the rental when we get back to Minneapolis."

I look dumbfounded, "We're driving back to Minnesota?"

She is already out the door, and I quickly follow. She opens the truck and throws her suitcase in. She unlocks the driver's door and jumps in, throwing her large purse onto the back seat. I open the passenger door and drop my briefcase on the floor and hop in. The parking lot has cleared as she heads toward the exit.

I say, "My suitcase is still at the Marriott. Can we pick it up?"

She replies, "Yes, I know how to get there, but after that, I'm at a loss of which way to go."

I grab my briefcase and pull out a Rand McNally Pocket Road Atlas. It's about the size of my hand and has a page for every U.S. state. I show it to my driver and smile. She gives me a look as if expecting such a thing from an engineer.

I say, "My name is Jim."

She replies, "I'm Deann. I guess we'll be together for the next couple of days."

Deann takes some back roads through neighborhoods to reach the rear of the Marriott. I guess she's had regular business trips to our new headquarters since the merger began. She drives under the canopy to the hotel entrance, and I hop out. I run into the hotel and up the three flights of steps. I open my room door and first stuff everything in the bathroom into my shaving kit. I throw the roller bag on the bed and toss in the shaving kit. I grab the shirts and pants on their hangers in the closet and fold them into a bundle to fit into the suitcase. I zip it shut and am out the door in less than five minutes. I try to find someone at the front desk, but no one is around. I leave my key and head for the waiting car—another thing to be straightened out later. I open the back door and toss in my roller bag. I move my briefcase to the backseat as well but keep the Pocket Road Atlas in my hand. I open it to page 33, New Jersey.

Chapter 3 New Jersey

Rand McNally Pocket Road Atlas page 33
11 September 2001

"Morristown is actually on this map," I say after I've been staring at page 33 for a few minutes. "It looks like we should take Interstate 287 South. Do you have any idea which way I-287 is from here?"

Deann looks at me with a questioning look. She turns and looks out the windshield. I feel she is losing confidence in my ability to navigate, much less get us to Minneapolis. I've always felt confident in my navigation skills. I want to explain that I am very good at directions, but here I have limited data. I have no starting point to reference, and I've not been able to study the problem.

I state, "I think we should go east. The Morristown dot on the map is to the west of the green interstate line. Which way is east?"

Deann continues to wait for directions. I twist my head around to locate the sun. It's behind us. I also notice that black smoke covers much of the blue sky on what I figure is the eastern horizon.

I say, "East is behind us. There looks like a major highway to our right. Let's get on that. There's a driveway ahead to our right."

Deann is happy to start driving. As she takes a right and heads for the driveway, we see a large DO NOT ENTER sign. She stops the car, "We can't go that way."

I reply, "No cars are coming. We can make it. It's an emergency."

Deann puts the car in reverse and backs into the parking lot, "Even if there is chaos all around us, we still have to follow some order."

I offer a half-smile. Is this really the noble thing to do? Can't one break all the rules in an emergency? Is there a difference between a crisis and a situation that's hopeless? Indeed, in a desperate situation, all rules of order are off. Do I interpret every sense of trouble, things not going my way, as a hopeless stage? A justification for outlandish behavior that will bring things back to normalcy?

I am awakened from my daydream by Deann's voice, "We can go out the back. There must be some roads that connect to that highway."

"OK," I stammer. "Let's keep looking for Interstate 287 South."

Deann makes a couple of left turns, and sure enough, we're headed toward an intersection into that major street. She turns right, and we immediately see a sign for the interstate. The right lane bends onto Interstate 287 South. We are the only car on the road.

"OK, how far do we go on this road?" asked Deann.

I study my little book, page 33. After a moment, I reply, "I think we should take Interstate 78 to the west. It'll take us into Pennsylvania." The numbering method of interstate highways offers logical help. Even-numbered roads travel east and west, while odd numbers go north and south. We need to find even-numbered routes to go west and odd-numbered to go north. Eventually, we'll find our homes.

After a few minutes on Interstate 287 South, we see a sign for Bethlehem, and I say, "That's the exit we should take, Interstate 78 West."

As we near the interchange, a memory haunts me. It's my father reprimanding me for not rushing to the Hoppie barn fire. Neighbors help neighbors, no matter how futile it may seem. I feel a need to take the east entrance and follow the freeway into the city. There must be a way to help. Suddenly both Deann and I gaze forward. Streaming on the crossing freeway is a convoy of ambulances. All with their lights flashing. There must be fifty of them, bumper to bumper, pedal to the metal. Although not needed, Deann slows and pulls onto the shoulder of the road. It's an act of honor to those hoping to help. After the last one passes, Deann begins to drive off. I feel there is nothing I could do that those first responders wouldn't be able to handle. There I am again, rationalizing my failure to take action and help. But the logic of the situation said it would have been useless anyway. You can't show up to a barn fire thirty minutes late. What's the use?

Deann takes the exit onto Interstate 78 West. I turn on the radio and scan till we hear a news report. The North Tower has also collapsed. Mayor Rudolph Giuliani calls for the evacuation of Lower Manhattan south of Canal Street. More than one million residents, workers, and tourists must leave the city. Frantic efforts are underway searching for survivors at the World Trade Center site. I wonder what the chance of surviving 100 stories of concrete and glass falling on you is? I feel those ambulances we saw won't be for survivors but victims. Why do I so quickly give up on hope?

After hearing the radio report repeat the morning's disaster, I ask, "How's the gas situation? Maybe we should stop around Bethlehem and fill up. I want to call my wife and let her know I'm heading home."

"You didn't call her?" shouts Deann. "While I was working out the plans for the car, I tried my husband and finally got through to tell him I was safe and would be driving back."

"I did leave a message," I sputter. "But she's not the most mobile these days. I suspect she may be spending the day in bed."

"She's not feeling well?" asks Deann. "Is she alone?"

"Our youngest son is in high school, and our two oldest are on their own. Bree works in the city, and J is at college in Wisconsin. Lately, Joan's been spending most days resting in bed."

"What's troubling her?"

"It's a long story."

Deann turns down the radio, "We have lots of time. Can you talk about it?"

"Actually, I haven't talked about it much."

I begin the story that we've agonized through for the past eleven years. It started on another Tuesday, in the spring when Joan physically could not muster the strength to get up. The kids headed to school, and I headed to work with her lying in bed. After months of urinary infection treatments and heavy doses of iron pills, the doctors scheduled an MRI test. At that time, MRI, Magnetic Resonant Imaging, was a new diagnostic tool for the brain. We had an appointment on a Saturday morning at the University of Minnesota's Medical Research Center.

Joan spent most of the morning lying inside a large torus as I watched from the control room. I was quite interested in the technology, having studied physics and designed and worked with superconducting magnets at one time. Two weeks later, we got the diagnosis. Joan has Multiple Sclerosis. Not a day goes by that I don't think of that disease, and not a minute goes by for Joan that she doesn't feel (actually the lack of feel) its impact.

Multiple sclerosis (MS) is a disabling disease of the brain and spinal cord (central nervous system). In MS, the immune system attacks the protective sheath (myelin) that covers nerve fibers, which leads to communication problems between your brain and the rest of your body. The disease causes permanent deterioration of the nerves. Because the brain is mostly a network of neurons, scans of the brain are used to diagnose and track the disease's progress.

Deann has listened in silence, staring at the road ahead. She frowns and breaks into my monologue, "I can't imagine what it would be like to live that way."

I agree, "It's unfortunate, but after the diagnosis of MS, one's life is mostly highlighted by the various treatments administered. The attempts to slow the incurable disease."

We ride together, lost in our thoughts. The most help I give Joan is to provide an excellent health insurance policy. We've so far not had to confront the financial consequences of seeking the latest care.

As I watch a series of billboards pass by, I say, "Hey, let's take the next exit. There are several filling stations where we can get gas and hopefully make phone calls."

Deann turns into the first gas station and heads to the one open pump. I hop out and start filling the tank as she strides into the store. I shout for her to toss me the keys, and I'll move the car after filling it. Even though there are hardly any cars on the road, there are many getting gas. We are not entirely sure of what is happening in the world. Our focus on getting out of everyone's way has left us a bit isolated.

Chapter 3 Pennsylvania

Rand McNally Pocket Road Atlas page 43
11 September 2001

I merge back onto Interstate 78 West. We are about to pass through
Bethlehem. "How about we drive for about an hour and then stop near
Harrisburg for lunch?"

Deann nods, "Didn't everything seem unusually quiet at that gas
station? It was eerie."

I reply, "The clerk didn't say anything when I paid for the gas. It was
like she was in a daze."

Deann says, "You know I can pay for the gas as well. I guess we're
both on expense accounts with the company."

"Sure. What are you working on, if I may ask?"

"I lead our marketing at the Home and Building Controls in Golden
Valley. Since the merger, we've been developing a joint marketing
strategy for consumer sales. We sell most of our home thermostats
through retail chains, and Allied has a line of products, most notable
Fram oil filters, that sell through these same stores."

I inject, "I wouldn't think these should interfere with each other."

"To the consumer, that's true. But to our customer, the retail chain,
they want a package deal."

"That shouldn't be that complicated."

Deann sneers at me, "Where do you work?"

"I work in our Technology Center. My group is split between the
Camden office and the Semiconductor Fab in Plymouth."

"Well, let me tell you, Mr. Engineer, there's just as much creativity
needed in marketing our products as making them. For instance, we've
had a sales agreement with Walmart for the past ten years. They
demand a price reduction every year. We said this was impossible, and

17

then they prepared an entire manufacturing plan on how they could reduce our costs, yes, OUR COSTS. They determined what materials and parts we were transporting to our final assembly in Golden Valley. They provided a schedule of how they would deliver those components as needed and then a calculation of the resulting savings. After those savings covered the price reduction they sought, the remaining savings were split 50-50. Every year they make more money selling our thermostats, and we make less."

"Why don't you tell them to buzz off?"

"They account for over fifty percent of the sales volume for that product. The other fifty percent is divided amongst all the other hardware stores nationally. If they didn't carry our brand, our product's sales would drop by twenty-five percent or more. Besides, the savings they have found for us increases our profits on the other fifty percent sales. So, in the end, we both win, but it doesn't seem completely fair. And now, as a combined company and our expanded product line, they have even more ideas for 'savings'." Deann raises her hands and wiggles her forefingers as she says the word savings.

I raise my eyebrows, 'Wow. I can see how this might be complicated. The retail store thinks of us as one company, but we run each business unit as a separate profit center."

"We've been at it for six months. The new agreement must be finalized by the end of the year. How about you? What were you doing at our new world headquarters?"

I take a deep breath and lean back into the seat. "We're reorganizing R&D for the new company. I was to be with my counterpart for the next three days working out project plans and funding for 2002."

Deann turns in surprise, "I thought that was decided when they took over last December."

"It was completed at the business unit level, but the corporate labs were given an extra year. We argued that our R&D center held a tremendous value, and it would devastate the future of the new company if we were closed."

"I never heard they were closing the research. They closed our Minneapolis corporate headquarters before the merger was even completed."

I shout, "That was no merger; it was a take-over. There was no official announcement on the corporate research centers."

Deann turns toward me with a questioning look. My outburst does not intimidate her.

I settle back into my seat and continue, "The merging of research was handled in a bizarre way. You recall, Allied Signal's Chairman, Larry Bossidy, stated the merger would boost Honeywell's annual sales above $20 billion and deliver $54 million in synergy."

Deann asks, "Synergy?"

I glace at her, "That's what you know as 'savings'," as I raise my hands and imitate her motions from before.

I quickly put my hands back on the wheel and continue, "$54 million is exactly the budget for our corporate research center."

"You have to give that guy credit for knowing what Wall Street wanted to hear…"

I cut in, "And what's going to work out especially well for himself."

I pause as Deann gives me yet another questioning look. I sense she sees this merger as a chance for her to win. I don't have that optimism. But I try to stay at least neutral in my expressions. I certainly don't want to come across as an old grouch, although I am probably twenty years older than her.

I continue, "Last November, fifty of us from Honeywell and fifty from Allied Signal came together for two weeks at a hotel in Phoenix. I had a two-room suite, but the TV room furniture was replaced with a conference table and an overhead projector. I hosted two to three meetings each day between two business units, one from our Honeywell and the other from Allied Signal, for five days. Oh, these were fun meetings. What engineer or researcher wouldn't enjoy sharing R&D results for the past few years and plans for the coming two years? We didn't identify many projects that one would say were an overlap."

Deann bites her lip and slowly mumbles, "Did everyone really participate openly?"

"Yes, for the first week at least. Each morning, at 8 am, we started with a standing meeting in the ballroom, all 100 of us. Dave Purvis, a corporate bureaucrat from Allied Signal, led the meeting summarizing progress and plans. Each evening, we gathered at 5:30 pm for a happy hour. It was a boisterous affair with many people shuffling around between standing groups. After six days, we had the Sunday off, and a few of us spent the day golfing."

Deann snickered, "How nice."

I stared ahead and said, "Yes, everything was quite nice, till the second Monday morning. Purvis announced we would repeat all the meetings from the previous week, but now we were to identify cuts in the R&D budgets that would total to, you guessed it, $54 million."

"Wow. That must have changed things!"

"That's one way to put it. Now each business unit questioned the other's projects. Where before, the results were considered new and interesting, now they were old and insignificant. Many times the meetings just stalled with only the speaker rambling on for fifteen minutes without a pause, and few listening."

"What did you do?"

"Well, I took the assignment seriously. I figured there were about ten meeting rooms like mine, so each should identify about $5 million in cuts. Over those five days, I tried to find a million dollars a day. As a result, I wasn't making any new friends, and behind the scenes, I sensed my loyalty to Honeywell being questioned."

"Did you still have the happy hours?"

"Yes, they were still hosted with free drinks and appetizers, but more of us were drinking hard liquor instead of beer or wine. The stand-up tables cordoned off either only Honeywell or Allied Signal people. The elimination of chairs to encourage circulation and interaction worked the week before. But once one feels under attack, there's a natural feeling to form a defensive group. Before long, we brought in chairs from the ballroom, and gang-like groups formed, dividing the room in half. By the end of the second week, if they'd given us balls, both sides would have engaged in a heartless dodgeball game. At night, groups of us Honeywell managers met to list which projects of theirs should be cut. A unified list of Allied Signal useless projects would serve to defend our own."

"Feelings must have been tense."

"Each morning, we were a bit refreshed and open-minded, but this evaporated quickly. At the stand-up morning meeting, Purvis's staff had collected project lists from our groups and showed a running total of the synergy so far identified. By the third day, we could see we were not on pace to reach the $54 million mark. Purvis's staff put added pressure on us room leaders to meet the goal. The two CEOs, Michael Bonsignore and Larry Bossidy, were flying in on Saturday to hear the results. Purvis was not about to tell them he couldn't deliver the 'synergy' expected."

I took my hands off the wheel and again repeated Deann's hand motions as I said, synergy.

"So I guess you came up with a list."

"Yes, there was a long list of projects that totaled to $54 million surprisingly. And we spent Saturday morning sitting in mass in the ballroom as Purvis's staff presented the details. However, in reality, no one had bought into these cuts, especially the managers directly impacted, and the new year started with almost no reduction in research staff."

"So you dodged that ball then?" said Deann, smiling at her reference to my earlier depiction.

I smiled back as I replied, "I guess we dodged that ball, but we still lost the game. I was meeting this week with our new Honeywell research directors to plan my group's future. My boss lost his job on the day of the merger, and I needed this week to secure mine."

Deann looks ahead and then behind our car as she says, "I don't think things are going to be too secure for a while. Anyway, let's stop for lunch. I'm hungry."

I was surprised that Deann would have a sense of insecurity. Was she talking about jobs or the terrorist attack? We already seem so far away from the problems. The roadway is vacant. I turn off an exit and am immediately surprised to find lines of cars waiting at the filling station. There are no cars on the road, but everyone seems to need gas. I pass these lines and turn left into a diner. It's almost 2 pm, and most of the tables are open. We take one where we can watch a small television behind the checkout counter.

We both order the lunch special with a coffee and then stare at the soundless television. We watch repeated images of the South Tower and then the North Tower of the World Trade Center collapsing. There are close-ups of reporters standing in front of the rubble. Another scene shows a reporter pointing to a western Pennsylvania map, and another shows smoke coming from the Pentagon in Washington, D.C.

As the waitress brings out the plates of food, Deann asks, "We've been traveling, what's going on?"

The older woman sets the food in place and replies, "It's airplanes. Two flew into the World Trade Center, one into the Pentagon, and now one has crashed west of us in Pennsylvania. All planes nationwide have been grounded, and the military is on high alert. Reports are that it's all part of a giant terrorist attack."

Deann and I sit in a state of bewilderment. We had just left the New York City area. Now it seems the entire east coast is under attack. The waitress is too shocked to talk further. She leaves the check and heads back to watch the television, craning her neck to look up as she sits at the counter. The cook comes out from the back and leans to watch the TV. He stares for a while but does not say a word. The waitress offers no comments as well. The cafe is in an entire feeling of disbelief.

Deann and I watch as much of the reporting as we can while finishing our meals. We split the check leaving plenty of cash for the bill and a tip. Deann heads for the door, and I follow quickly behind. We don't say a word as we leave, and nobody notices.

Chapter 4 Detour

Rand McNally Pocket Road Atlas page 43
11 September 2001

Deann asks for the keys and says she'd like to take over the driving. The roads are almost deserted, except for the long lines at the filling stations. Our tank is still three-quarters full. We head west on the interstate.

I break the silence, "I feel like we're on a get-away."

"Yea, like we were involved in those attacks. It's like we're running away."

"But in plain sight, and no one sees us."

Deann raises her head, "Hey, you didn't call your wife."

I reply, "I've left two messages, but she must be having a bad day. Our youngest son will be home from school in a couple of hours, and they'll then know I'm OK and heading home. Hopefully, they won't worry."

Deann looked over at me, "Don't you worry about leaving her alone? Especially if she's having these bad days?"

"After eleven years, any sense of panic is gone. Actually, almost any sense of any kind is gone. Happiness, longing, anticipation, anxiety have played out. We mostly live on hope. In fact, that's the main word used by the dozens of doctors who've cared for Joan."

"Dozens of doctors?" exclaimed Deann!

"At first, she had several urinary infections. They'd get one cleaned, up and another would start. It seemed she'd lost sensation in her urinary tract, so things were building up and not being relieved."

"That's weird. When I gotta go, I gotta go, that's it," Deann stated to the windshield.

"With MS, it's your nerves, and it's not just a loss of feeling, but also your energy. Everything seems to weigh more. By the summer of that first year, Joan was having trouble finding the strength to get out of bed on any day. A new doctor decided to administer treatments in a hospital. They were able to monitor her vital signs as they injected super doses of steroids. The main objective was to disrupt her immune system. In MS, it's your immune system that's eating away the insulation on the nerves. As the insulation disappears, the electrical signals short out to the fluids and tissue and don't get through. There were five days of intense steroid doses. At one point, the nurse asked me to go to the hospital pharmacy and pick up the treatment. They made me sign several papers of my obligation to deliver this liquid bag for treatment, of course, which I did. But as I was riding up the elevator, I figured this must be worth thousands on the street."

"How big a dose was it?"

"I estimated it was about one thousand times a normal dose. Well, the effect was almost immediate. Within a couple of days, Joan was walking the halls and in good spirits. Within a week, they sent her home, but she had to continue intravenous steroid treatments every day for a month to taper off the addiction they induced. It was the beginning to years of daily support from many of her friends."

"Were there side effects?"

"Well, it's not good to shut down your immune system. Certainly, athletes do it to gain bulk and strength. Several of Joan's friends joke with her to take up bodybuilding. Although this gave her energy, it didn't renew any strength. She's had more than a dozen of these treatments over the years with diminishing boosts. They've recently determined that these massive steroid treatments produce more of an hallucinogenic bump and don't actually deliver any restoration to the nerves. And the shutting down of your immune system is not good. The immune system has evolved to defend the body from invasive diseases."

"Our immune systems should be better than that. It should be able to sort between internal and external threats."

I pause and then mumble, "I'm not sure anything is good at that."

Deann points at a road sign shouting, "Hey, we're on Interstate 81!"

I see the sign and am in disbelief. I study my pocket road atlas and, sure enough, see that I-78 blends with I-81. I say, "We're heading south."

I search the map, but it's hard to read as the printing is misaligned across the centerfold. I then say, "It looks like we can take Highway 30 West at Chambersburg. Let's look for that exit."

Deann takes a deep breath and blows the air out as a statement of her doubt in my navigation abilities.

We take the exit and follow the road through the town. Again there is little traffic except for long lines at the gas stations. We have almost half a tank, so we should be good for a while. I say, "This Highway 30 will take us into Pittsburg. That might be where we can find a hotel for the night."

"And fill-up the tank," Deann declared. "But maybe we should avoid large cities. They all might be terrorist targets."

The highway is quite curvy, weaving through small farm fields and across wooded hills. Although the map makes no note of this, I think we are crossing the Appalachian Mountains. The drive comprises being emersed in the woods only to witness beautiful valleys of irregular patterned fields. Some of the fields have been harvested, and others lay in wait. Although the area looks well sculpted by humanity's hand, there is no humanity to be seen anywhere. It's like everyone has deserted. A strange feeling comes to me. I can't quite place it. It's not fear. It's not unhappiness. It's loneliness. Deann is beside me. She's maybe not a friend, so to speak, but she's undoubtedly my traveling companion till we get to Minneapolis. Where is this feeling of loneliness coming from?

Suddenly we come over a small hill, and there are two police cars with flashing lights blocking the highway. Deann slows and coasts up to them. One of the officers walks toward the car and shouts that the road is closed and we have to go back. Deann rolls down her window and asks for directions to Pittsburg. The officer stands erect and shouts again that the road is closed. Maybe our New York license plates are not helping. Deann works the car into a Y-turn. He continues to glare at Deann till we are headed back in the direction we came.

Deann wonders, "Do you think Pittsburg's been attacked?"

I say, "I'll try to find some news on the radio."

I scan both the AM and FM bands using the digital seek button. I'm reminded of my Uncle Charlie and how he came to dislike his latest new car. He claimed he could no longer run the radio as they had removed the two familiar knobs that had served for decades the three controls needed for a radio: on, volume, and tuning. In their place were nearly a dozen buttons that poorly performed those necessary features. I now realize what he had known all along. As I pushed a seek button, the numbers on the radio rolled ahead and then stopped. A staticky station came on, but it was difficult to understand. I pushed the button again, and the search continued. The radio found a few stations playing music on the FM band, but none offering a news stream. I kept pushing that button. At times we would catch a few words from a newscast, but then a turn in the woods or a going over a hill would turn it into static. I eventually turn the radio off. Somehow in the middle of Pennsylvania, we are alone.

I study the map, "We're headed back toward Bedford. We can take Highway 220 South. Maybe we should go around Pittsburg."

Deann heads back toward Bedford as we watch for Highway 220. We catch it just before entering the town, and Deann turns South. We're now driving down one of those Appalachian Valleys we'd been crossing before. It is very scenic but much slower traveling as it's not a divided highway. We pass a sign that says we're entering Maryland.

Deann looks at the sign and asks, "Maryland? Are you sure we're heading home? It seems like we are going in circles."

I study my map and I reply, "Yes. In fact, we've just crossed the Mason-Dixon line. Before the civil war, it marked the separation between slave states and free states."

Deann comments, "That's a past I'll never understand. It was a disaster."

"Actually, the Civil War is not considered a disaster," I state. "Disasters are over quicker."

"That's not true," returns Deann. "Disasters run on their own timeline. Who knows when the one we're in will end?"

"Yes," I reply. "I was hoping to put this merger behind me this week, but that's not going to happen."

Deann looks at me with a puzzled look.

I swallow and peer at the tiny map. "It looks like there's a piece of Maryland we cross and then we'll be in West Virginia. South of the town we can take Highway 50 west."

The sun is getting low in the west and I wonder about searching for a motel. I can't pinpoint our location on my pocket road atlas as there's not enough detail for that. Suddenly we cross a river in a small town and see a huge sign saying, "Welcome to West Virginia".

The few street lights in the town have come on. Deann says, "I think we should try to find a motel before it gets too late. I'd also like to get something to eat, and everything looks pretty deserted right now."

Deann drives slowly for a few minutes as we both search for any sign of a place to stay. We reach the end of the town and head into the darkness. After a few more tense minutes, we both notice a tall sign reading Keyser Inn. Deann quickly turns right and drives the half block to turn left into the motel's parking lot. She pulls in front of the overhang entrance. Only a couple of cars are in the lot, and we wonder if we'll be able to get rooms.

Deann hits the bell on the counter. She hits it a couple more times. An older woman comes from the back, "Welcome. How can I help you?"

Deann answers, "We'd like two rooms for the night."

"Well, I've got plenty. Not many people are traveling today. Everyone's canceled and seems to be headed home. Isn't it a tragedy, what's happened in New York?"

Deann says, "We were there, and now we're trying to get back to Minnesota."

The woman stares at the two of us as if we were aliens. Who knows what must be going through her mind. She stammers, "How will you pay for them?"

Deann opens her purse and pulls out a credit card. She says as she hands over the card, "I'll pay for my room with this, and Jim will pay for his."

We fill out registration forms, and the older woman hands us keys. My room is down the hallway to the left, and Deann's is to the right. I guess the owner didn't want us conspiring in the night to blow her place up. As Deann walks away, she turns back toward the clerk asking, "Is there a place to get something to eat nearby?"

The woman replies, "Just head back into town, go north and turn right on Piedmont Street. There are several bars in the downtown area that will serve some type of food. The bars don't close for anything; holidays or national disasters."

We both walk out to get our suitcases and agree to meet back at the car in fifteen minutes. I immediately call home. Tim answers the phone, and I ask them how they're doing. He says things are OK, and he's cooking some dinner. He carries the portable phone up to Joan, who's still in the bedroom. She's glad to hear my voice, and I'm relieved to listen to hers. For the past ten years, our relationship had become more practical than intimate. Most of our interaction centered around having something to eat twice a day. Even though she hardly ever went out into public, Joan still worried about her looks and even her weight. She'd always had a great figure, but this was not easy to maintain laying around all day.

Last June, we had celebrated our twenty-fifth wedding anniversary by attending her nephew's wedding in Wisconsin. It was the first time that Joan spent the entire day openly sitting in a wheelchair. It was for some of her relatives, the first time Joan plainly admitted her malady. It required a tremendous amount of personal energy to get turned out in her new dress, attend the wedding and bride's dinner, and then the reception. Normally, we would be the last to leave these celebrations. This time we were the first. We departed even ahead of the grandparents.

I told Joan I had seen the two towers on fire and that everyone wanted to leave the office. I was lucky to find another Minneapolis Honeywell employee who found a rental car that we are now driving back. I should be home in less than two days. She said she was becoming furious about these attacks, and these terrorists must be dealt with severely. I am surprised by this attitude, as Joan was hardly one to show any ill will toward anyone. Years ago, she told our children that if she hadn't gotten married, she would have been content to be a nun. As I hang up the phone, Joan hopes I will travel safe and be home soon.

I'm a little late getting to the car and offer to drive back into town. I spot a gas station where the lines don't seem too long. We eventually fill the car and head toward Piedmont Street. Before long, we find a saloon with beer signs lit up in the windows. We take seats along the bar near the front windows. A few others are sitting at the other end of the bar. They look like regulars as the bartender leans on the bar talking with them. I wave over the bartender and ask if there is a local beer we should try. He brings us two bottles of Yuengling beer and says he can cook us a frozen pizza. I find the pizza not that bad as I enjoy it with several of these Pennsylvania beers. Deann doesn't seem quite as pleased but eats her share and, after two slices, also seems to like the beer. There's a television above the bar showing a newscast. I ask the bartender if he could turn up the volume.

A series of reporters outline the disasters as they happened. There were four commercial airplanes hijacked and turned into weapons. Two hit the World Trade Center, causing both towers and the center building to collapse. A third dove into the Pentagon in Washington D.C. A fourth crashed in a remote area in Western Pennsylvania. That explained the closed road we encountered. The number of fatalities was unclear, certainly all the airplane passengers, but probably many more who were trapped in the buildings. Deaths no doubt totaled in the thousands. The President has declared a national emergency and intensive investigations are underway to locate any further terrorist plots and neutralize them.

The small group at the other end of the bar is not paying attention to the news reports. I guess they've seen these reports over and over. What happened has happened, and one is left with one's own thoughts of what it will mean for the future. It's interesting when disaster strikes, how quickly we accept that it happened, but how long it takes to absorb it and then decide how to move on.

Chapter 5 West Virginia

Rand McNally Pocket Road Atlas page 25
12 September 2001

Deann and I grab a cup of coffee from the lobby and head for the car. Deann has changed clothes. She wore a blue dress suit with a white blouse yesterday. Today she has on casual clothes, jeans and a light maroon pullover golf shirt. Her soft blond hair seems to be longer today. Yesterday, she must have had it tied up, but I now realize how little I had paid attention. She's pretty and, I think, has probably the same makeup as yesterday, but I wouldn't swear to it. I do notice she's changed from dress to tennis shoes. I have on the same grey slacks as yesterday but with a different dress shirt. I'm not wearing a tie today. Deann still seems tense, but not quite as much as yesterday.

We decide to drive for a bit before stopping for breakfast. Deann takes the first leg of driving as I study the map. A few miles ahead, we will catch Highway 50 which will take us into Ohio.

Deann says, "Hey, I forgot to ask if you got in touch with your wife yesterday."

I finish taking a sip of coffee, "Yes. She's doing OK. No emergencies anyway. She's been following the twenty-four-hour news coverage of the attacks, and I was surprised how angry she is about them."

"She knows more than we do," commented Deann. "Even though we were right there, we sure don't have any idea of what is going on. I just hope we can find a way home."

Soon a sign for Highway 50 comes up, and Deann turns west. It feels good to have the bright sun behind us. I start looking for a place to have breakfast. Tall trees and occasional houses line the road. My map doesn't show the road having so many slopes and curves. It seems Deann is testing each turn for maximum traction, but I don't say anything. We work our way over forested hills and rocks and sail along the valleys until the road heads over another mountain. Just before we pass over a branch of the Potomac River, a sign says we are again in Maryland.

Deann slows down and shouts that we are going east, not west. I assure her we are going in the right direction. We continue along the peaceful tree-lined highway, and as we reach the top of a hill, the landscape opens to farmland. Before long, I see a sign for a café off the road to the right. We turn at an intersection called Redhouse and travel about a mile north to find a café in the middle of an animal farm. Again the place is empty, and we're left to our own concerns. The eggs and bacon with freshly made bread are incredibly comforting.

I take over the driving, and as we return to Highway 50, I notice a church on the right that I'd missed before. I slow down as we pass the small Redhouse Lutheran Church with a graveyard that takes up most of the lot. I ask Deann, "Are you Lutheran?"

"Yes. My mother was a true Minnesota Lutheran, an expert on hot dish cooking."

I laugh out loud and sputter, "I grew up Catholic, and we're better at beer fests!"

Deann slightly smiles. I add, "So are you good at cooking hot dishes yourself?"

Deann's smile disappears, "My mom's not happy that I don't go to church."

I offer, "Maybe you should make her a hot dish."

She turns to me and snaps, "That's enough about religion."

I turn right onto Highway 50.

Before long, I'm surprised to see a sign saying we are entering West Virginia. I try to hold back my emotion, but Deann spots the boundary notice as well. She says, "Let me see that little book."

I have it in the pocket of my dress shirt and hand it to her. I say, "We're on page 25."

She opens the book and squints at the two-page map that includes Maryland, Delaware, Virginia, and West Virginia as one white area. As she squints to read the closely held book, I say, "It must have taken a lot of meetings to get the boundaries of these states so screwed up."

She doesn't look up from her studies but says, "Must be ancestors of those trying to organize our new research centers."

I frown and hope she notices. But she's pulled the tiny atlas closer to her eyes. I say, "I think it's a good idea to avoid big cities, which might be the likely sites for more terrorist attacks."

She nods in agreement and puts the book down. As we drive, the sky seems bluer than usual.

She says, "I'm not good at reading maps, and this can hardly be even called a map. I have no idea where we are on this."

"It's better if you know where you've been. Then you can figure out where you might be."

She sneers at me as she hands back the book. She thinks for a minute and then says, "That might work for a lot of things."

I blurt out, "It certainly has not worked for treating MS!"

Deann exhales slowly before saying, "I didn't know there were treatments for it."

"Yes, there are three. They're called the A-B-C drugs. We're lucky because we live in Minnesota there's quite a bit of research that goes into the study of multiple sclerosis. There is no complete understanding of what causes someone to get MS. Some theories connect it to living in northern latitudes and being exposed to hundreds of viruses during those cold months spent mostly inside. Minnesota, Wisconsin, and Michigan have the majority of cases. Even people living in Arizona that are diagnosed often spent some of their teenage years living in a northern climate."

"I grew up in Minnesota and don't know anyone who is affected."

"It's not a contagious disease. It's an immune disorder that affects less than 1 in 1,000 people in the US."

"Your wife isn't very lucky."

"Well, that never seemed the case for the first 37 years of her life, but now some of her luck is that we live in Minnesota, where most of the MS medical research is based. In fact, over the past ten years, three drugs have been introduced specifically to treat the symptoms of MS. Joan hasn't had the best of luck with these drugs, but there's always hope that another will come along."

"They didn't help her?"

"In some cases, they made things worse. The first drug ever approved for the treatment of MS was Betaseron, the B of the A-B-C drugs. It was approved in 1993 by the FDA based on a two-year study where Betaseron injections delayed the time to a second flare-up. MS patients around the world were ecstatic that there was finally some treatment, some hope. Joan was one of the first to receive the drug. We attended a training course on the medicine and how to administer it through injections. I remember we practiced on an orange giving it shot after shot with a syringe we refilled with water. Injections were to be taken at precisely forty-eight-hour intervals. It seemed easy. I did the first few for Joan in her butt, but she gave them to herself before long. I guess I was a little rough, having first learned to give penicillin injections to baby calves and making sure the needle got through that cowhide. The calf never gave you a second chance. Eventually Joan moved to use her thighs as the injection site. With every other day injections and a body that didn't heal itself very well, her body became peppered with red dots. She kept going until she had a huge relapse and ended up back in the hospital. It had just been a few months since starting the Betaseron, and her reaction was not consistent with the drug's claimed side effects. The next team of doctors took her off the Betaseron and administered the massive steroid treatment. Within a week, Joan was back home and at least able to take care of herself and even make a few meals for us."

"You said the steroid treatments were not good."

"Yes, but they were the only thing that Joan responded to, and quickly. She asked for them. She even begged for them. Then in 1996, a second drug was approved, Avonex."

Deann adds, "The A drug."

I smile at Deann and quickly turn back to watching the road. This talking is good for me. I feel alert, alive, telling a story that I've not ever put into words before. I've only played it through my mind, over and over, day after day.

I continue, "Yes, the A drug. This drug only required injections once a week, but they were more painful. However, there were 48 possible side effects listed, with one especially catching my attention, depression. Betaseron had only listed 11 common side effects."

"Even 11 seems like plenty. But 48? And this drug was approved."

"People were desperate for some hope. Whereas Betaseron was thought to increase the time before a second flare-up, Avonex would extend the time between flare-ups. Again we attended a training class. They were upfront and near the end of the session, admitted the mechanism of action by which AVONEX exerts its effects in patients with multiple sclerosis is unknown. This drug was only taken once a week and administered as pre-filled syringes. The drug was advertised to deliver a 37% relative reduction in the risk of accumulating disability. "

I stopped my monologue for a moment and explained to Deann that at one point during these drug treatments, I had started reading the technical papers on the research. I had searched for the quantitative findings that the FDA used to approve the drug. Each study seemed to invent new methods to develop the statistics.

I continued, "So this A drug seemed like a fit for Joan. Since 1996, Joan had had five significant relapses involving some combination of problems with balance, coordination, eyesight, bladder function, fatigue, weakness, numbness, and sudden needle-like pains. Each time it took longer to come back to some level of ability to get around the house on her own. By now, she'd given up the idea of ever running marathons again."

"Joan was athletic, but still this disease knocked her down?"

"Yes, mostly she was a runner. She ran every day, usually early in the morning before the kids woke up. She even ran in the Frozen Half Marathon that was part of the St. Paul Winter Carnival. The kids and I would wait for her to finish in Rice Park. Now that was a test of endurance and determination that was certainly beyond me. I admired her for such an achievement."

"I like to run, but never once thought to try that Frozen Marathon. Did you ever run yourself?"

"I ran a few mornings with her, but Joan left me in the dust. I was always more of a sprinter than a long-distance runner."

"That helps get away from disasters, but maybe isn't so good at avoiding the next one."

I turn and smile at Deann. I think I know what she's getting at, but I'm not sure, so I continue, "After six months taking those weekly injections of Avonex, Joan was having multiple complications. She didn't just seem weak, like everything was weighing 100 pounds, but also what I came to define as sad. One morning she had a tremendous weakness and we headed for the hospital. Again yet another set of doctors got involved and stopped the Avonex treatments. Joan didn't respond to any other treatments, except the month-long, over-the-top steroid doses. This time the recovery took longer and the doctors put her in a Care Center to gain enough strength so she could take care of herself."

Deann burst out, "I've told everyone I will never go to one of those places. Once you're in, it's impossible to get out."

"Joan understood this exceptionally well. One important thing is that you eat all your meals and have regular bodily functions. Well, the steroids don't give you much of an appetite, so she quickly devised a way for me to eat her three meals a day. After a few days, the nurses were quite surprised at her appetite and the use of the toilet and readily put forward the paperwork for her release. I'll never forget having to carry her to the bedroom and having friends come by several times a day to help her stay alive. But she was in better spirits and, after a week, could get around the house again. Even if her strength wasn't back, her clever wit had returned."

"So her mind was good?"

"Yes. Her mind was like her young self. It was the inside of her body that was 100 years older. Some call this the 'best-looking' terminal disease."

Deann cuts in, "But the drugs were not working."

"A year later, another drug comes out, Copaxone."

"The C drug."

"Again, we went to a training class. This drug only listed twelve possible side effects. Injections were to be given every day. With so many injections and so little healing, Joan made red spots across her thighs, the top of her butt where she could reach, her stomach, and the backside of both arms. It didn't look good, but Joan persevered with hope. It was her only hope at the moment. But as time went on, her personality changed. Her clever wit disappeared. She only saw the worst in things. Everyone was treating her poorly. She created fictitious spats with neighbors that she hadn't even talked to lately: people attacked our kids, saying bad things about them. I was targeted because I wasn't supporting these stories enough. She settled into a depressing state of mind."

I stopped for a moment. I couldn't say what I had thought at that time. Was it the disease itself causing this behavior change? Or the sedentary life that left one in a chair all day? Or the loneliness of not being able to explore? Or the day-long dribble from talk television that over and over told one how to take action, to establish your own perfect world? I never found one reason more responsible than another. All seemed to play a part in this depression. Somehow, I couldn't say these words out loud.

Deann looks at me wondering what is distracting me. "Did you talk with the doctors about this?"

I reset myself, "Yes. I called her primary care doctor and also her current MS specialist. I told them about this personality change. They said they would cut the dose in half, but the drug had shown a more than 30% improvement in delaying flare-ups, and it best be continued. I decided to find out more about these studies. I found the papers describing the studies for both the Avonex and Copaxone. The Mayo Clinic in Rochester led the studies for the drug companies. They used some metric called the Kurtzke Expanded Disability Status Scale (EDSS). The EDSS is a scale that quantifies disability in patients with MS and ranges from 0, normal neurologic exam, to 10, death due to MS. Most patients in the study have a score below 3. I believed Joan was closer to a 6 than a 3. After testing hundreds of patients for two years, the average EDSS score for the people taking the drug increased around 30% lower than those on the placebo. So the paper concluded that the drug produced a 30% improvement in delaying MS. When I looked at the actual data, it seemed that about 10% had a significant improvement in this metric, about 85% had no change, and 5% were dropped from the study, some due to attempted suicide."

"Attempted suicide!" exclaimed Deann.

"Yes. But the paper abstract summarized the data as a 30% improvement across the entire group. I showed the paper's details to the doctors, who had, of course, never read the full paper, only the abstract. I said they should administer the drug to identify the 10% who have a significant improvement and drop it for the other 90%. Of course, this idea would not be profitable for our medical system. I was brushed off as someone not familiar with medicine. I pleaded that they watch for the 5% and address this immediately. I felt that Joan was in that 5%. Maybe fortunately, she didn't have the strength to do much to injure herself. But her lashing words were destructive enough. In my opinion, the search for hope had turned into hate. Anyway, the next set of maladies ended Joan's use of this drug."

I couldn't go on. I couldn't talk anymore about this. I needed a break. Why was I dumping all this on Deann? Was I even saying this out loud? I wasn't sure.

As I look over at Deann, she seems to be lost in thought. I distract her, "Hey, I think we are now in Ohio. Should we look for a place for lunch?"

We pass a sign for the city limits of Athens. I first stop for gas, where the station does not have any lines. We then stop at a café another few blocks down the road, which has just two cars in front. I guess those belong to the cook and the waitress.

Chapter 6 Ohio

Rand McNally Pocket Road Atlas page 40-41
12 September 2001

It seems our waitress has been pent up all morning waiting for someone to come into the restaurant. She sets down two cups of coffee at the counter before we can even say hello. She has her reddish hair pulled back into a bun and has on a spotless, tight-fitting white dress. An apron with large pockets is tied around her waist. She says, "Please sit here. It's so nice to see someone today. I'm Carol."

Deann replies, "Thank you. Could we see a menu?"

She quickly replies, "I'd suggest our special of chicken-fried steak with mashed potatoes and green beans. It's ready to go."

Deann and I look at each other and nod. We both turn to Carol, who waits, not expecting to take a different order, and agree. She turns and shouts into the kitchen, "Two specials."

Carol walks to fill two glasses of water and says as she sets them in front of us, "So where are you coming from?"

I think that's an interesting question to start a conversation. I guess it's less nosy than asking where you're going. Deann answers, "We were in New York City yesterday."

Carol freezes and slowly looks at first Deann and then at me as she says, "Oh my god."

Deann says, "We're on our way to Minnesota. We both live there."

I add, "We were able to see the World Trade Center as it was on fire and left when the towers had fallen. We don't know much about what caused it."

"It was airplanes!" exclaims Carol. "Terrorists highjacked airplanes and flew them into the buildings. I've watched those two towers collapse so many times, I've turned the TV off. Each time I see it, I think of another person--a secretary, an accountant, a vendor, a delivery person bringing coffee and donuts, a salesman, a mother, a father, a fireman—

who is now buried in that rubble. All were people like me, just doing their job and hoping to get home in time for dinner. Authorities say they won't know who's missing until they don't show up at home."

Carol grabs a handkerchief from an apron pocket and dabs her eyes. Deann and I mourn with her.

Carol clears her throat and continues, "They don't' know exactly who and how they did it, but they turned these planes into weapons. I can't even imagine what it was like for the people on those planes."

Deann asks, "Do they know much about which flights they were?"

"Yes. The two planes that hit the World Trade Center left from Boston and were both flights headed for Los Angeles. The plane that hit the Pentagon had taken off from Dulles Airport also headed for LA. The plane that crashed in Pennsylvania had taken off from Newark headed for San Francisco."

Deann almost drops her cup and spills most of the coffee onto the counter. Carol grabs a rag from her apron pockets and swipes it up. Deann looks at Carol, "One of my colleagues was leaving from Newark yesterday morning, flying back to the west coast, but I don't know exactly where. I think she was headed to Los Angeles."

"Let's pray to God she was," comforts Carol. "There're no survivors from any of those airplanes. The Pentagon attack didn't kill many people, but they estimated thousands died in the World Trade Center. Firefighters were caught as they headed up a hundred flights to put out the flames blazing from the airplane's fuel. It's horrendous, and the entire country is in shock."

Deann says, "It's been eerie driving with everything appearing in perfect order, the buildings, the forests, the fields, but there are almost no people to be seen."

"Everything is closed worrying about more attacks," added Carol. "Airports are closed. I think any non-military airplane flying above the U.S. will be shot down."

I mumble, "That's why the sky seems so clear and blue. No jets are disturbing the atmosphere. No contrails."

Deann says, "Yes, things seem orderly, yet there's probably panic hiding everywhere."

"Everyone expects another attack," remarks Carol. "The President has the military on high alert worldwide."

"We've been avoiding the big cities," I say. "We thought that Pittsburg had been attacked because we ran into a roadblock."

"But it must have been due to that plane crash," adds Deann.

"Avoiding big cities is a good idea, terrorism or not," states Carol. She turns and grabs two plates that appeared on the pass-through window to the kitchen. As she sets down our food, she says, "Although last year, a TV show portrayed our town as the Scariest Place on Earth."

"Athens, Ohio?" I utter.

Carol frowns and continues, "The Athens Lunatic Asylum opened after the Civil War and treated thousands of patients, more with mental than physical ailments. They had devised some pretty horrendous treatments for these diseases. When one looks back at the therapies for incurable patients, it's hard to tell who was crazier, the doctors or the patients. It was all done in the name of hope."

"Hope is often the banner that desperate people use to do desperate things," I mutter.

Deann and Carol look at me as I study my food and cut off a bite from the chicken fried steak.

Carol continues, "Well, the whole world is giving us hope. Every nation has denounced these terrorist attacks and stands ready to support the defeat of terrorism, even Libya and Iran. The only country that has not denounced these attacks is Iraq. They hailed the disaster as 'the operation of the century which the United States deserved because of its crimes against humanity'."

"Wow," states Deann. "This might not end well for them."

We finish our meals as Carol fills us in on more history of the town and its strange doubling of size while the university is in session. We split the check, and each leaves a worthy tip. Deann takes over the driving as I study the map. We can follow Highway 50 till Chillicothe and then catch Highway 35 toward Dayton. As we drive, we both comment on the deep blue sky and the lack of airplanes.

I break the silence and ask, "Say Deann, what does your colleague do, the one that was flying out of Newark yesterday?"

Deann takes a quick look at me and replies, "She works in business development at one of the Allied Signal offices in Los Angeles. She's helping us in avoiding counterfeit products from production in China."

"I didn't think we manufactured much of our home products overseas. Don't you have that completely automated factory for the round thermostats right there in Golden Valley?"

"Yes, we produce all of our products in the U.S. But our new company thinks they can increase profits by off-shoring our manufacturing. It's one of the ideas that Wall Street especially likes about the merger."

"Yea, and another is the closing of our R&D center. Why all of a sudden is Wall Street running our company?"

Deann looks over at me, "I wasn't around in the 80s, but people say that's when engineers ran the company, and Honeywell lost over $500 million in one year."

"Yes, and I was part of that. Well, I mean, I was part of the study that generated the lessons learned. Anyway, I want to point out that today's most reliable and profitable products came from those times. The accountants were too short term in their planning."

"Well, the new accountants have some short-term profit goals to meet, and they're pushing to send our manufacturing to China. Allied Signal has been doing this for years with their products."

"And if that works so well, why did they have to dump their name so fast and take ours?"

Deann ignores my question, "Manufacturing in China does cut costs, but it takes some attention to maintain a level of quality. The real hidden problem is counterfeiting. It's quite common that the factory managers agree to a very low production cost and will run the factory for two shifts. However, a secret third shift runs occasionally, and your product is then made but all with the same serial number. Those units are boxed with the same official labeling, but we don't account for them. These counterfeit units are sold as part of standard shipments, and that payment goes to an unknown account. My colleague explains that the factory price stays low as long as you let them have a piece of the action on their own terms."

"Wow, sounds like quite a balancing act."

"I'm starting to believe everything goes out-of-balance as we push to be global. The more we push to make every place follow the way we have done it in the past, the more resistance we see."

I add, "And feel." I wonder how many people are like our waitress, Carol? Have they lost hope? What do I feel now? Do I feel like I'm running away from something, some big disaster? I guess I am. But what is it exactly I want to get away from?

We are traveling on Highway 35 as we pass a sign listing Dayton sixty miles ahead. I point at the sign, "We'll take this highway through Dayton and continue on it into Indiana."

"Do you want to stop in Dayton?" asks Deann.

"No, I'm good," I reply. "Unless you need to. I've spent enough time in Dayton already."

"Really? It seems out of the way."

"It's home to the Wright-Patterson Air Force Base, which encompasses the airfield Wilbur and Orville Wright used in 1904. Among other Air Force groups, the Sensors Directorate develops new technologies to detect the enemy and eliminate its ability to hide or threaten our forces. I was here the day the Challenger Space Shuttle blew-up, January 28, 1986. It was also my youngest son's second birthday."

"You have a knack for taking part in history. Remind me not to travel with you again," Deann snickered.

"A colleague and I were meeting with the Air Force describing some new fiber optic sensors we were developing. We wanted them to join, and fund, a flight-testing program with us. They seemed interested.

We finished the morning-long meeting about 11:30 and decided to stop for lunch before catching a flight back to Minneapolis. When we went into the restaurant, much like the one we visited in Athens, it was deadly silent. There were a few more people, but the place was as if frozen in time. My colleague and I slipped into an open booth and waved for a waitress. She slowly walked over, and I ask 'What's going on?'. She simply says the Space Shuttle just blew up and drops two menus on our table. There's a small television above the cash register, and we become fixated on it like everyone else."

"I was in college then and didn't find out about it till that evening."

"It was especially sensitive to Dayton because so much of the city's history involves aircraft design and safety. The citizens took the disaster as a personal assault. You could feel their disbelief and sadness at the restaurant, at the airport, even on the highway."

Deann remarked, "The same as I feel now. It's like the world has slowed down, but we continue to race through it faster than ever. There's a closeness that I'm missing. We are the fastest thing moving, but it still seems we are being left behind."

I ponder these thoughts for a moment. I realize there's yet another issue plaguing my unrest. I begin out loud, "These disasters make one think of fate. In the case of Challenger, there was a series of events that contributed to the explosion of the solid rocket boosters. First, the launch had been delayed several days for various issues, but partly out of an abundance of caution, because it was the first space flight with a civilian on board, a high school teacher from New Hampshire. They finally agreed to launch on the coldest morning. The cold caused an O-ring to fail, causing the solid rocket booster to leak fuel. A frozen chunk of fuel got sucked against the hole and blocked it. Then just at about the worst possible time and altitude, the shuttle hit the largest wind shear ever experienced, and the chunk was snapped off from blocking the hole. The hole grew and eventually caused the entire rocket to explode."

Deann looks at me in bewilderment, "How do you know all of this?"

"After any spacecraft or aircraft trouble, the entire industry engages in understanding and diagnosing the source of the problem. It's an amazing experience. Everyone forgets rivalries and shares insights and hypotheses. It becomes a worldwide engagement of the scientific process. Within hours, the most probable causes have been identified. The collective knowledge of our aerospace technology is a human marvel."

"I didn't know you were so involved in the aerospace industry."

"To me, that's the main reason Allied Signal bought us."

"It was a merger, at least that's what the shareholders were told."

I ignore Deann's comment and continue, "Between Allied Signal and Honeywell we produce nearly 80% of the components needed to build an airplane. Some have joked that all we now need is aluminum to build airplanes ourselves."

"But what about our other businesses, Building and Industrial Controls?'

I look at Deann, "Well, isn't that what you're working on? How to bring those businesses into the Allied Signal business model?"

"Yes, and it's been interesting for me."

"Well, on the aerospace side, interesting isn't the word I'd use. But I have to admit; it's a time that one would expect consolidation. The Military is about to award a fighter jet contract that will last for decades. The Joint Strike Fighter may be the last fighter jet that I see developed. I've judged my career by the development of aircraft, especially fighter jets. My first job was with McDonnell-Douglas, now Boeing, in St. Louis. In four years, we brought out four new aircraft. Since then, I've had a hand in the design of every aircraft built by Boeing, Airbus, and Lockheed-Martin. Presently, there are almost no new planes on the drawing board, and after this disaster, the need for new versions may be significantly delayed."

I look at Deann. She's focused on the road and seemingly in her own thoughts. I ramble about my memories of the early days of my career. The first project was the speed brake on the F-15. The Eagle is a twin-jet, all-weather tactical fighter aircraft designed specifically for the Air Force. The speed brake, made of composite material, could be snapped out and back into the airstream. It provided the pilot the capability to change airspeeds during dog fights dramatically. It was the first use of composite materials in a production aircraft. We had lots of trouble making that structure not crack apart from such a dramatic shock.

The second project was the lightning testing of the Harrier jet, or AV-8B as designated by the Marines. The Harrier used thrust vectoring from the engines for vertical takeoff and landing. The Marines crashed all 40 they had just purchased from the British. We developed a lighter version using composite materials. Since this was for Marine's use in any weather, it was possible the aircraft would take lightning strikes. There was concern that the composite material consisting of graphite fibers and epoxy would not provide the same level of shielding as a metallic surface, and they were right. We built a charging tower that could generate a one-million-volt lightning strike. The inside of the wings lit up like a Christmas tree when stuck. This space also served as the fuel tank, and a lightning strike most likely would result in an explosion causing the wing to come off. We never actually tested that, but we did lose one plane during flight testing in western Missouri during a thunderstorm.

The third project was the windshield testing on the F-18 jet fighter. The Hornet was designed explicitly for the Navy and aircraft carrier operations. An issue was that the plane might be more suspectable to bird strikes and the windshield's durability had to be validated. We built a gas-propelled gun that shot chickens at the windscreen. After a few material changes, the windshield was approved to withstand a bird strike. Our practical testing method was widely copied. We helped an Irish company test train engine windows. Every window they tested failed until we reminded them to defrost the chickens before firing.

From there, I went on to be part of numerous developments ranging from the control of ejection seats to missile navigation. I had worked with dozens of customers on hundreds of new product developments. But as we pass through Dayton, I'm reminded that these days are coming to an end. The Military is about to award the production for the Joint Strike Fighter. It is a single design that can be modified to meet Air Force (high speed dogfights), Marine (rapid escapes from tight spots), and Navy (carrier landings) needs jointly for sixty years. The belief is that a single design with multiple configurations will save money. But I feel this would parrot the joke of the horse and the camel. A camel is a horse designed by a committee. No one would expect a camel to be used as a race horse, a work horse, and trick pony by changing the saddle.

The competition for this contract was intense. My research group may be the only group in the world that supported the two remaining competitors, Lockheed and Boeing. I had to keep the two development projects separate inside my group because of competitive secrecy. For Lockheed, we were working with the design of the lift fan for vertical takeoff and landing that would be an insert for the Marine's version of the jet. For Boeing, we were developing a new laser-based air data system for precise aerodynamic controls. As part of the quotes, we had to provide pricing of the products and support, showing savings, out to the year 2060[2]. One could think it required tremendous experience to create such a quote. But according to Allied Signal's thinking, no experience was needed at all since you'd renegotiate everything anyway.

As we pass through Dayton, the emptiness on the streets indicates the grieving from yet another aerospace disaster that these citizens are especially taking to heart. I can also sense the phone lines buzzing with hunches and conjectures on how yesterday's tragedy could have happened. I am in disbelief that Allied Signal can let all the experience of my group with all our contacts just be pushed off. Then again, maybe I've outlived a career in aircraft research and development. The company may no longer need researchers but rather business experts like Deann to renegotiate and quote the next orders.

We see a sign welcoming us to Indiana.

---

[2] The Joint Strike Fighter contract was awarded on 26 October 2001 to Lockheed Martin, whose X-35 beat the Boeing X-32. One of the main reasons for this choice appears to have been the method of achieving STOVL flight, with the Department of Defense judging that the higher performance lift fan system was worth the additional risk. When near the ground, the Boeing X-32 suffered from hot air from the exhaust circulating back to the main engine, which caused the thrust to weaken and the engine to overheat. Wikipedia, https://en.wikipedia.org/wiki/Joint_Strike_Fighter_program

Chapter 7 Indiana

Rand McNally Pocket Road Atlas page 19
12 September 2001

After plenty of squinting and close-up gazing at the Indiana map, I say, "This Highway 35 will take us to the town of Logansport. It seems a good place to stop for the night. It'll be almost dark by the time we get there."

Deann glances at me, "OK. How far is it?"

I look at the map. According to the scale, the width of my thumb is about fifty miles. I measure the distance as three thumb widths and reply, "About 150 miles. It'll probably take a little over three hours. We're averaging less than 50 miles per hour because of having to slow down through so many small towns."

"I think going through these small towns is better than trying to figure out what trouble there might be in the big cities. Small towns are friendly."

We weave our way through thousands of farm fields, and dozens of what Deann thinks are friendly villages. At times we feel like we are the last survivors on earth. We talk about work and the new company some but mostly ride in our own thoughts.

As we enter the south side of Logansport, there are no signs offering directions to a motel or even downtown. I say, "I think we should take a right ahead."

Deann looks over at me and asks, "Why?"

"Because I feel downtown is to our right."

"I'm not sure we should trust your feelings."

I glance at Deann, who is watching the road. I can't really argue with her comment. I'm not sure even I should trust my feelings. I seem to have too many feelings or none at all. I can't tell.

I utter, "I can't argue with that. The map is too small to see any detail of this town. But I still think we should take the next right. I don't see a hotel ahead or even a place to eat."

I point with my left hand at the next intersection. I then motion with my index finger to go right. She slows and makes the turn. We follow this Humphrey Street for several blocks till it dead ends. We turn around, and I point to the right at the first intersection. Deann takes a deep breath as she follows my directions. She's biting her lip again.

I spot a stop sign two blocks ahead. I point right, and as soon as we make the turn, I notice a bar ahead on the left. I point for Deann to turn into an empty parking lot on the right, across from the bar, "Let's park in this lot and walk over to the bar. At least we can get a beer. Maybe they even have Yuengling."

"And some information on a motel nearby."

We walk across the deserted street, which looked like it would typically have a stream of traffic at this time of day: people coming home from work, others heading out for an early dinner, trucks getting in one last delivery, students heading home from their after-school activities and others on their way back to school for a sporting event. But this road is empty for blocks in the north and south direction.

The Dutch Mill bar is certainly not empty, and the row of regulars filling the stools all turn to look at us as we enter. Deann waves shouting "Hello" as she heads for a table behind where two couples sit at the bar. The two women sit together, and the two men have pulled back their chairs to talk as a group. Deann takes a seat at the table facing them as I grab the one next to her where I can watch the front door. I had learned this on a trip to Mexico one time. If you aren't sure of your surroundings, you should make sure you face an exit. Did Deann have the same uneasy feeling? Why did it bother me? What is it that's bothering me?

The bartender peeks through the two women and Deann orders two Yuengling's in bottles. The bartender doesn't flinch at the request and quickly returns. He asks one of the women to hand the beers over to us.

The brunette-haired woman grabs the two beers as she steps off her stool. She says, "Here you go. Welcome. I'm Irene and this is my husband Boyd. And this is Phyllis and Dale."

Irene looks like the spark plug for the group, while Boyd appears relaxed and always ready to enjoy life. Dale, as the opposite of Boyd, has a full head of dark black hair. Phyllis sports a styled permanent hairdo while Irene lets hers fall with shoulder-length curls. The men have clean-shaven faces while the two women display dangling earrings with noticeable face make-up. All four wear almost matching slacks and button-down shirts. They appear to have known each other for years and probably have spent more than a few hours each week on these stools. Just how they situate themselves gives the impression they're ready to absorb anything new that enters the bar.

I grab a beer and nod at each of them, raising my beer slightly. Deann says, "Thank you. I'm Deann and this is Jim. It's nice to meet you. We haven't met many people the past couple of days."

Irene says, "We figured pretty quickly you're from out of town. What brings you here?"

I cut in stating, "The attacks in New York!"

The four of them fixate on me and then look to Deann for an explanation. She sneers at me and then begins, "We both work for Honeywell in Minneapolis. We were, for different reasons, at our new world headquarters in New Jersey for meetings. We could see the World Trade Center on fire. Both of our meetings were canceled…"

Irene cuts in, "That's one way to put it."

I want to clarify that we were not in the Trade Center but could see from afar. How close does one have to be to a disaster to consider it happened to you?

Deann is not taken back and continues, "Well, yes, everyone wanted to find safety and especially secure their families. We were left on our own and, through some luck, were able to borrow a rental car which we're driving back to Minnesota."

Phyllis says, "So you've been on the road for the past two days."

I realize Deann's being put on the spot and try to take over some of the interrogations, "Yes, we left yesterday morning and have been avoiding large cities, thinking if there are more attacks, that's where they would target."

Boyd asks, "So you don't know much about what has happened?"

I reply, "We can't get much info from radio stations because the reception keeps changing. We did see a bit of television last night when we stopped for dinner."

"Every channel has broadcast nothing but news on these attacks. So far, there have been four airplanes involved, and our skies are open only for military use. No one knows if there are more attacks planned, and the terrorists are only hiding till airplanes start flying again," exclaims Irene!

Dale says, "It's like we're under an armed guard."

"But it's self-imposed," cuts in Irene.

Phyllis adds, "The news just keeps repeating the live filming of the towers being struck and then collapsing. Everyone wants to know who did this and why, but so far, all they can do is count the dead."

Deann asks, "How many have died?"

Irene replies, "At the Pentagon, over 100 were killed, and they know the four airplanes had 265 passengers."

"Some of those were no doubt the terrorists who took over the airplanes," inserts Phyllis.

Irene continues, "And in New York, they don't know. So far, they've recovered over 100 bodies, but most can't be identified. There're reports of thousands posting pictures and visiting hospitals looking for their loved ones that didn't come home last night."

The four of them fall silent. They show a feeling of sadness that Deann and I hadn't felt so far. The people of Logansport are grieving. This grieving is connected between couples, between friends, and no doubt extends across the country. Deann and I each take a sip of our beer.

Are we only to be detached observers of this disaster? Or can we still be participants?

Boyd breaks the silence, "Last night, President Bush called the attacks evil, despicable acts of terror and declared that America, its friends, and allies would stand together to win the war against terrorism."

The bartender approaches and asks if anyone needs another drink. All six of us nod yes.

Deann changes the conversation to local topics. I understand her success in business development. She has a way to relate to people she doesn't know. Maybe even be of help to them. I study the four locals. They must be retired, and I wonder about the regularity of this happy hour visit. Even a national disaster won't interfere with it. Or maybe it's the reason to get out of the house. These four seem frozen in time. But hasn't the entire nation been frozen for the past two days? Is it time that has frozen, or just our minds? Disasters don't stay frozen in time for very long. What triggers a release to move forward in one's mind? What triggers these four to decide when to go home for the night?

Deann elicits numerous pieces of information from the four citizens. Some combination of them worked for banks, construction firms, and the local power company. Their children have grown and left town. The town's population has been on the decline for ten years, except in the past two years it's growing. Migrant workers, mostly Mexicans, have been flocking to the area to work at the pork processing plant. The town even has a radio station that only plays Mariachi music. It looks like they're going to stay. Small towns in Indiana are changing. Logansport has one nationally significant entry in the record books. It was the first high school in the country to have a mascot, and I add maybe the most unusual. It is the cartoon character Felix the Cat. The cartoon character, Felix, isn't so popular today, but in the 1920s, during the time of silent films, this character was a celebrity. Its human mannerisms reflected something people recognized in a relative or friend, or even themselves. As a symbol, I believe Felix was more motivational for the speech competitions than football games. When Boyd and Dale played, they had winning sports teams.

At some point, Deann orders a chicken sandwich, and Irene talks me into ordering the breaded tenderloin. Dale says it is the best in Indiana, which Boyd clarifies as being the biggest. We enjoy our sandwiches and share a basket of fries. Deann obtains recommendations for a motel as we finish our beers. We are both surprised to see how dark it is outside as we leave.

We head north, crossing the Wabash River into the downtown. If we hit the Eel River, we've gone too far. Who'd want to go near Eel River? We take a left on the first one-way street, Market Street, and follow this for a mile or so. The Super 8 motel looks as if every room has been kept vacant just for us.

Chapter 8 Illinois

Rand McNally Pocket Road Atlas page 18
13 September 2001

We are up early and grab a coffee from the lobby. We decide to drive for a while before we stop for breakfast. We'll gain an hour today when we cross into Illinois. Deann takes the first leg of driving and heads back toward the downtown. She follows Market Street, taking the parallel Broadway Street during the one-way portion, heading west. It seems like a major road, and we follow it as it curves through the town. Near the west edge of town, I notice a sign for Highway 24, straight ahead. This road can take us as far as Peoria, Illinois.

After about an hour, we stop at a café in Wolcott, a small town that fits into the grid of farm fields. We say good morning to the few in the café, but for the most part, people don't seem ready to go about their everyday business just yet. If we hurry, we can get to our homes before dark tonight. Maybe these disasters will look different tomorrow, hopefully.

Deann continues the driving. I sense she's feeling anxious for the ride to end. As we pass the sign welcoming us to Illinois, I ask, "Did you talk with your husband? What's his name, Gary, last night?"

"Yes, what's his name Gary, is working hard. He's glad I'm on my way home. He was ready to come get me if needed."

"Has he been affected by this national disaster?"

"Not really. He started a used car business a couple of years ago. He can spend hours detailing a car, and once he's finished, it will sell quickly. He makes a car looks so good that people jump at the chance to buy it."

"Well, watching the roads the past couple of days, maybe we won't need cars much anymore."

"That's not going to happen. Things will be back to normal before long. But I'm not saying that we're going to forget about this disaster."

"Disasters, in the long run, affect more the way we think than the way we act. I worry about the change our company is going through and the fact that my career has run out of projects. I'm haunted that my wife can hardly lift a spoon to feed herself. But what exactly can I do about any of it?"

Deann asks, "How's Joan doing?"

I reply, "OK. As well as can be expected, I suppose. I talked with her some last night. She was able to get into the kitchen yesterday and make a dinner for our son."

"Can she get out to buy food?"

"No. She has a laptop in the kitchen and uses a new food delivery service, Simon Delivers. She can select almost any packaged food and even produce as if in a grocery store, and they will deliver it in insulated crates the next day. The toughest part for her is to get the crates from the front steps into the kitchen."

"She has a laptop in her kitchen, how modern."

"She's quite proud of that and shows it off to all her friends. I'm not sure this online ordering is for everybody, but it is important for us. Tim and I get meals, and Joan has a sense of normalcy, of being a mother."

"Does she have many normal days?"

I pause for a moment. Do any of us have normal days? Will we ever have normal days? What is a normal day anyway? I reply, "Well, for her, a typical day is being able to do what you did the day before. At first, we went through so much worry and concern and unknowing, even if the next day might bring a sudden change. We had completely forgotten what life was like before. We had to plan each day new considering the energy or accessibility available for that day. Eventually, we just gave up planning, taking each day as it came, one after another."

"That's what work's like these past few months. Maybe this is preparing me for being a mother."

"Joan, of all things, is best at being a mom. The school bus stop was in front of our house. Every day, she would be out there helping the kids if they forgot something and letting them in to stay warm. After some point, every kid in the neighborhood had depended on her for something. She had a way to sense their fears and address them."

"I've heard that most people with MS live in fear of flare-ups where the disease becomes crippling again."

"Yes, and that's what those A-B-C drugs are advertised to address. But as I said before, those didn't work for Joan, although the doctors, with their kickbacks from the drug companies, refused to accept that fact. It wasn't till the more serious health problems arose that they gave up."

Deann jerks to face me and shouts, "What!"

"She's had three bouts with cancer."

"Cancer? Three times?"

"The doctors will never admit it, but we figure it resulted from the drugs messing with her immune system, especially the huge steroid treatments."

"But you said they were the most helpful to her."

"Yes, she does not regret them. In fact, I think she'd like to have more if she could talk a doctor into giving them again. She just wants to have more energy, even if it comes from a hallucinogen."

"You don't have to answer this but has she tried some recreational drugs?"

"No. She's not interested in any treatment outside what a doctor would administer. As much as the medical system has failed her, she will only follow their advice. Four years ago, they discovered a lump on her left breast. They did a lumpectomy and saved the breast, but it was quite deformed. A year later, a Mayo Clinic doctor diagnosed a growth on her thyroid, and a couple of weeks later, surgeons removed her thyroid. And last year, another lump was detected. This time they did a breast removal and reconstruction from her belly fat. They shaped up the left one to match the new one and tattooed an areola around a bunched-up nipple."

Deann starts to blush, "You make this sound like it's car repair."

"Yes. In some ways, doctors are much better at physical treatments. They can cut and stitch because they've learned to do this extremely well and have excellent tools. But when it comes to solving problems involving chemistry, it just seems a big guessing game. Maybe much like most of us. When disaster strikes, we plan and can execute physical action, but the problem may be better solved with diplomacy and time."

"You mean eating right and exercise instead of fistfights."

I smile at Deann, "That's not a bad way to think of this."

Deann doesn't smile back, "Well, in this case, this disaster, these attacks, no one's going to go for more talk. They will expect action and lots of it."

"I'm sure our military has already picked plenty of targets. They have the best tools in the world for massive destruction, and I should know. I've been involved in developing many of them. But what if this terrorism is more like MS than cancer? Surgery is not the solution."

"But taking a hallucinogenic is not either."

I'm surprised at Deann's hawkish attitude. We enter the city limits of Peoria. I guide Deann to take Interstate 74 West toward Moline, where it will connect to Interstate 80. I use my thumb and estimate it's less than 100 miles to Iowa. We decide we have plenty of gas to get that far and then stop for a late lunch.

As Deann is maintaining maximum speed on the Interstate highway, she exclaims as she passes a sign, "Hey, we're going through Galesburg. One of the seven Lincoln-Douglas debates was held here in 1858."

I'm surprised at her enthusiasm and attempt to show interest, "Really? I don't know much about that."

"I'm a bit of a history buff, and it formed a turning point for politics in the United States. Abraham Lincoln, the Republican nominee, and Stephen Douglas, the Democrat, competed for a state legislature seat.

Lincoln challenged Douglas to a series of debates, and the two eventually agreed to hold joint encounters in seven Illinois congressional districts, of which Galesburg was fifth on the list. The format was more like separate campaign speeches than a Q&A. However, the meetings took on a nationwide following because the topic debated, slavery, was important across the country, not just in Illinois."

I cut in, "A house divided against itself cannot stand!"

Deann takes her eyes off the road to glance at me as she says, "You know some history as well."

"Not much. But that idea has always resonated with me as we debate which new technologies we should pursue, often at the cost of displacing the old. We must forecast what is possible with the technology, but forecasting is mostly educated guessing. Suddenly opinions are more prevalent than facts. The emotional arguments cause divides between groups, even between individuals that have been friends for decades. We have one research center and one set of labs. Some competition is always good, but at some point, we have to leverage everyone's ability toward a single goal."

"Isn't that what we were both doing at headquarters?"

I smile at Deann with a puzzled look. Maybe I'm not looking at things from afar as I should be.

Chapter 9 Iowa

Rand McNally Pocket Road Atlas page 20
13 September 2001

We ride caught in our own thoughts following the divided highway.
The world still seems very quiet, and now we are passing it at freeway
speed. The atlas map doesn't have space for labeling the freeways
surrounding Moline, but one looks like a north bypass, and I guide us
onto that. We know we've hit Iowa when we pass over the wide
Mississippi River. We catch Highway 61 North and drive for a few
miles. I spot a Cenex gas station ahead, and we take the exit to the
right.

After filling up, I ask the attendant where we might get a quick lunch.
He directs us to go under the highway, and there'll be a Happy Joe's on
the right. They have a lunch buffet of pizza slices that is quite popular.
The big lunch rush is just about ending, so we may have poor pickings,
but we won't have to wait long. Deann isn't too excited about this
lunch idea. I take over the driving and follow the advice given.

I've been driving for about an hour as we enter the south side of
Dubuque. I hadn't planned the next leg and ask Deann if she could
look at the map and determine if we need to change roads. She grabs
the tiny book from the center console and finds the page for Iowa. She
can't find Dubuque, and I suggest she look on the right border of the
state. We're paralleling the Mississippi River. Soon she spots it and
pulls the book close to her nose.

Deann says, "It looks like Highway 52 would take us toward
Minnesota. Otherwise, we're going to end up going into Wisconsin."

"Hey, I know Highway 52. That'll take us to St. Paul."

 As we enter the town, I take the turn-off for 52. We weave through the
one-way streets of downtown Dubuque and are soon headed out of the
city. The scenery has changed to more of a hilly and wooded
landscape. It's a pleasant change from the miles of farmland we've
passed for most of the day.

"The plane, The plane!" I almost shout.

Deann looks over at me, "You don't seem the type that would be a fan of Fantasy Island."

I reply, "I'm not, but there is a plane in the sky." I point out a contrail high up against the blue sky. "Maybe they've opened the airports."

"Or it could be a terrorist divebombing the IDS tower."

"Do you always think the worst?"

"I never used to, but the last couple of days have given me plenty of time to realize things aren't so good in the world. Maybe it's time we put ourselves first and keep out all those foreigners."

"Did that group of retirees make a point with you last night?"

"They are not happy about losing their town, the one they built and dedicated their lives to."

"One mariachi band radio station doesn't mean they've lost their town."

"No. But hearing people not speaking English and grade schools teaching in Spanish is not what they're used to. The town represents Americana. Hey, the idea of school mascots originated there. The old ways were good enough for their parents and their grandparents, so why should they have to change?"

I try to keep my eyes on the road as I say, "How can anyone stop change? We live in a connected world. When there is so much imbalance, things are pressured to move. If you've noticed, Minnesota's added a Mexican radio station every time a tornado comes through town. There's an added need for construction, especially roofing workers, that is best filled with these dedicated and a bit desperate people. It's like a power supply, as the potential difference increases, no matter the resistance, a measurable current will eventually flow."

"Since most Honeywell products are electrical, I know what you're saying, but life's not as simple as a circuit. Electrical circuits don't have a feeling, for instance."

"Yes, working for Honeywell. What are you feeling these days?"

Deann hesitates and then turns to look out the side window as she says, "I'm feeling pretty low."

I'm surprised at her answer and give her a questioning look. If she's feeling low, then where am I? Maybe it's this melancholy ride that's getting to us. We've either been lost in our thoughts or talking about unhappy situations that, for the most part, are out of our control. We certainly don't know much about these terrorist attacks, but it seems to have put most of America, even the smallest, isolated towns, on a defensive hold. And between us, we can't see what opportunities, if any, there might be in the future. Indeed, the more I listed the treatments and consequences of multiple sclerosis that Joan has endured, the less I felt any understanding for what lay ahead. Are we just to be at the mercy of these situations? Should we be doing more than just trying to get home? What is help?

I reply, "I think you're a good fit for this new company."

"I've been one of the first to take all the new training programs. I just completed becoming a black belt in the Total Quality Management program. I'm now an expert at using spreadsheets and putting numbers against some made-up categories."

"You know quality used to mean meeting precisely the customer's needs. Now it's a scorecard on some fictional metrics. I started the green belt training, as mandated of all managers, but our class didn't finish. We had a hard time coming up with metrics that we could score and then use for improvements. Developing new products is a very chaotic process. It's not like we're manufacturing the same device every day. Statistics work best when the process is dealing with a bounded set of uncertainty."

"It's the same for business development. But we worked through the exercise and came up with a plan. No one knows if the plan will make things better, but it's a plan."

Another issue I have with this new company strikes me, and I say, "They have a strange process for raises and promotions if you ask me. Everyone in each group is totem poled."

Deann adds, "Yes, we do that as well. We rank each team member from top to bottom, and the top 10% get the biggest raises and the bottom 10% are told to find different jobs."

"That again doesn't make sense if one's been managing a group properly! I've been advising and working with each member to find where they can contribute the most. I want to think that every member in my group will win Honeywell's' highest technical achievement award someday. If I had ten Nobel Prize winners, I'd still have to fire one of them."

Deann looked at me and said, "In business development, we don't have to worry about Nobel Prize winners."

I laugh out loud, "You're a good fit for this new company. You're clever and find a way to make the best of things."

"Maybe there's going to be some good opportunities for me. I think the company has been too technology-driven in the past. Now it will be more market-driven."

I cut in, "You mean more bean-counters and fewer nerds. It's the nerds that drive innovation."

"That's not true. Innovation is the combination of an invention and then commercialization. Commercialization can add many new twists to a product, such as open up a new market or an adjacent use."

"That sounds like Black Belt wishful thinking."

"Wishful thinking is better than not thinking." Deann nods and smiles. She seems quite content with her thoughts.

The elevated road that cuts into the hillsides allows Deann to gaze far down into the Mississippi River valley. I focus on the road, but the curvy road doesn't allow me to see very far ahead. I come over one hill and spot a small sign for the Bily Clock Museum. To visit it, we'd have to take a three-mile detour off this main road into the town of Spillville. I've heard of this museum because I've had a hobby for a long time designing and building clocks. However, I work with electronics and LED's to measure time and display it in an interesting way. These two brother farmers, Frank and Joseph Bily, worked with wood and purchased the mechanical movements prevalent at their time.

In 1946 they gave dozens of pendulum clocks to Spillville, never to be sold. The standout works are The Apostle Clock where the Twelve

Apostles appear on the hour, The American Pioneer History Clock, and a clock commemorating Charles Lindbergh's historic flight. Someday I hope to see what they accomplished over the forty years of building clocks. I've been at it for thirty years so far, but I doubt my clocks will make it into a museum for posterity.

Within thirty minutes, we pass a sign stating we've entered Minnesota. I blurt a joke as I look into the rear-view mirror, 'When entering Iowa, remember to set your clock back ten years!'

Deann smiles and replies, "Maybe instead, you should think of setting a clock ahead ten years."

I wonder, am I able to do that?

Chapter 10 Minnesota

Rand McNally Pocket Road Atlas page 28
13 September 2001

This Highway 52 will take us to the south side of St. Paul. I don't know this part of the city very well as I live on the north side, but Deann knows and states that 52 will cross Interstate 494 which will take us to the Minneapolis-St. Paul airport. Both of our cars are parked there.

Highway 52 follows the western edge of the Mississippi River Valley. The road cuts through small forests and crosses slow flowing streams, with glimpses to the west of the flat, expansive prairie that has been squared into farm fields. We enter the city of Rochester from the south.

As we pass through the west of town on the four-lane freeway I point to the right, "You can just barely see the top of the Mayo Clinic. It's about a mile east of here."

Deann comments, "I've never been there, but I know when people are very sick, that's where they go."

"Joan's been there. They were the ones that diagnosed her thyroid cancer, but the surgery was performed in Minneapolis. They also were part of several studies on the A-B-C drugs."

"People really trust their work."

"They earned that reputation by being open and welcoming. In the 1880's the frontier doctor, William Mayo, was joined by his two sons, William and Charles, and they soon opened a hospital. Instead of being secretive and protective of their skills the Mayo doctors took on partners and visiting medical staff whose skills complemented their own. Doctors, after returning from Rochester, spoke of attending the Mayos' clinic. The term clinic has edged away from being recognized as a place to learn in favor of a place to be treated. However there are many ailments that should be approached as learning instead of in-and-out treatments."

Deann looks at me and says with a sadness I hadn't expected, "Joan's for instance."

I pause and consider my thoughts as I pull behind a semitruck going the speed limit. I turn to Deann, "Although that is how I feel, Joan does not think of it the same way. She's desperate for any help."

"She needs hope as well!"

"I'm of no use at either help or hope."

Deann looks sternly at me as she says, "Certainly, not many of us are doctors, especially those willing to experiment and study a complex disease like MS. But everyone can offer hope. What were you doing at headquarters? What have we been doing the past three days? We're really of no help, but there still is hope. It's hope that's kept us going. There's thousands of people hoping to find their loved ones alive."

"Last night on TV, I saw all those posters plastered on every wall and fence in New York City. The bodies they have gotten from the rubble are not identifiable. It's a worse disaster than I could have thought."

"The real challenge with any disaster is dealing with the aftermath. How we react? How we approach moving on?"

"I'd like to put up a poster for Joan. I'd like to find the one I married."

"That's crazy," Deann shouts!

I'm still following the semi as her voice seemed to have changed. I hesitate and then gather myself to say, "So you think I'm not facing the reality of this corporate merger?"

Deann looks over her left shoulder and quickly replies, "I didn't say that. But…"

I cut her off, "But it is true. I traveled to Allied Signal's headquarters…"

She now cuts me off, "Why do you keep saying Allied Signal? It's all Honeywell now!"

"Yes. That is true. I've been hoping I can save my group, my own job."

"But you've said your job is gone anyway. Your expertise has run its course."

"I'm not that old to be forgotten, to be passed over."

"What did you hope to accomplish this week? Your boss's boss and your boss have been given severance packages. Our former CEO has been fired and …."

I cut in, "What a setup. After the merger last December, our CEO, Bonsignore takes over. But six months into his rein the losses that Allied Signal had accumulated overwhelmed our profits and after two quarters of reporting losses, Wall Street had him out in two days. Then of course, Bossidy gets his old job back, but now with a clean balance sheet."

"Corporate take-overs are messy. Just like terrorists attacks and incurable diseases. There's winners and losers."

"Mostly losers," I inject! "And I don't like being one! I'm not used to it."

"Let's hope none of us ever gets used to disasters," stated Deann. "We're never going to have all the answers."

"I guess that's what I'm looking for most, honest answers. There's more honesty, more answers in a terrorist attack than a corporate take-over or being struck with an incurable disease. I'm searching for the truth."

"But what do you do when the truth can't be found?"

"You don't cover it up with misleading statements," I cry out!

"That would be lying," smirked Deann. "Do you think our management is lying when they won't offer funding? Do you think the doctors are lying when they administer the next treatment? Do you think the terrorists are lying when they dive airplanes into skyscrapers?"

I stutter at Deann's directness. I reply softly, "No. They're mostly focused on attacking a problem. I hate to think that terrorists are like doctors. Then I add smugly, "But maybe they're not that much different than Wall Street tycoons."

Deann smiles, "Diseases have victims. Corporate take overs have victims. Terrorist attacks have victims."

"The major difference is we've been dealing with MS for years. The corporate merger has gone on for months and the 911 attacks just days."

"But do you know any better of what to do in dealing with any of them?"

I stammer, "MS is an incurable disease where one suffers for twenty years and then starves to death. Corporate takeovers and terrorist attacks have the chance at more promising outcomes."

"Terrorist attacks are not in the same category as corporate takeovers. The world will certainly not see it that way."

"I'm not sure, anymore, how I see things."

"How lost are you?"

"You're right, of course. My problems are minor compared to what's going on in New York and even my own home. Living with death is devastating. The will-power and energy it takes for Joan just to visit with friends for an hour is more than I use in a week. It's time to accept the obvious. If still in one disaster, you're not sensitive to another. It's hard to separate them. The new one just blends into the existing one."

"You see everything as being only your problem. There is support that one can offer to the other as they die into a denial and retraction from life, waiting for things to get better on their own. One needs another to pull them out of the muck. It's very important."

"When Joan's disaster hit, there was a lot of crying at the beginning. It's mostly from not knowing. Eventually the crying gives way to…"

Suddenly my thoughts are cut off by a memory.

I'm lying on the couch. I've been there for several days. My eyes are inflamed. It burns when I urinate. Now my ankle and wrist have swollen into softball sized abscesses of excruciating pain. Joan is crying on the phone with her mother that I won't see a doctor. Her mother is not one you would call to cry with. After pleading for another half-hour I agree to visit a doctor. She immediately starts making phone calls. It takes weeks for several specialists to diagnose that I've developed a case of Reiter's Syndrome touched off from a devastating food poisoning left over from a business lunch. The recovery takes years involving dozens of drugs and hospital visits.

Deann gives me a puzzled look. I say, "I had a medical situation twenty years ago. I fought my way out of it."

She questions me, "Did you?"

I hesitate, take a deep breath, and then say, "Actually, Joan was there. She faced the situation and never gave up. She pulled me out of the muck."

"And now she's not able to do it again."

I ease my foot from the gas pedal to look at Deann, "It's not that complicated is it?"

"In the situation you're in, you should enjoy every day. After dealing with this, with you, I know it's time I enjoy every day. I'm going to be happiest gal when I get home," Deann divulged.

I smile at her and nod. Let's fight this disease. Let's fight this takeover. Let's fight these terrorists. In that order. Can I be of help? I will be a provider. Joan has faced her disaster with dignity. I should hope to have half that much poise.

We stop for gas just before the freeway that runs past the Minneapolis, St. Paul airport. Deann takes over the driving. She's expecting to be accused of auto theft. I wonder as well. We ride in silence as we enter the massive airport complex. We are the only car on the road. We're not that familiar with the rental car return in our own city and I point out turns and directions watching the overhead signs.

As we enter the parking ramp and spiral up to the third level, Deann asks, "How do you think the car rental place is going to react?"

I shrug my shoulders.

We see the entrance to the rental car return. We are the only car to be seen. As she crosses over the one-way tire piercing strip and slowly drives through the empty lot, three workers dressed in the rental car company outfits burst from a small building and sprint toward us. They are jumping and shouting and high-fiving each other. Deann stops the car and rolls down her window. A young blond woman runs up to the window and shouts, "We are so happy to see a car!"

A guy running around the back of the car adds, "AND YOU!"

Deann mumbles, "You're not mad?"

The woman smiles as she raises her arms, "Oh my god, NO! We have a hundred people waiting for a car so they can get back to their homes."

She turns to the third guy who has been circling the car on a dead run, "Ryan, go call the first name on the list. Tell them we have a car!"

She then says to Deann, "Please pull ahead to the front." She walks beside the car as Deann coasts ahead. She asks Deann to pop the trunk and if there is anything wrong with the car. Deann says no and the woman jumps in the driver's seat as soon as Deann exits. The guy following the car has pulled our bags out and set them aside. I collect my briefcase and especially grab the tiny Road Atlas that guided us the past three days.

As I approach Deann who is standing beside the bags, she asks the young man, "I need to pay for the car. We brought it from New York."

He states, "Wow, New York. Well, we've only been told to get any cars we have on the road as soon as possible. Somebody will straighten out the fees and car locations once we get through this disaster."

By now the young woman has sped off with the car. The young man asks, "Do you need any help with your bags?"

Deann says, "No thank you." She reaches into her purse and pulls out a business card to hand to the young man. He takes it and runs toward the small building.

Deann and I walk side by side toward the stairwell. We say goodbye on the landing. When we came, we parked on different levels.

Afterword

Honeywell soon promoted Deann.
I was 'let go' in 2002.
The U.S. invaded Iraq in 2003.
Joan passed away in 2010.
New Jersey established a September 11 memorial in 2011. The **Empty Sky** memorial reflects how people near Newark remember that day.

Acknowledgements

As most projects, there are a number of people and organizations that were instrumental in bringing this story to life. I list them in no apparent order and this book is as much theirs as mine:

Nancy Blake
Jane Sandberg
Randy Markward
Karen Leivian

These e-books and paperbacks by T H. Harbinger can be found through Amazon books.

The Electricity of Life

A Historical Novel based on the true story of Otto and Viola Schmitt and their role in winning World War II and later establishing the medical device industry of Minnesota.

13 Stories from Living in Germany

Whereas the most famous diary about Germany was from a young girl hiding from Germans, these stories are all about trying to find them.

Flying High with Consequences

A Historical Novel based on the true story of Professor John Karl and his Earth's magnetic field mapping research leading to the development of frac sand mines in Wisconsin.

The Archaeus Project

A Historical Novel based on the true story of a group of specialists who secretly work under the cover of a mansion in South Minneapolis to model a Human's Sixth Sense.

Only in Fargo: A Collection of Short Stories on the Simplicities of Life

Short stories on the daily life in the fictional version of Fargo. Every day the simplicities and complexities of life create experiences that lead to the telling of stories.

Gyro Landing

A Historical Novel based on the true story of the scientists and engineers who dedicated their careers to the precision controls that made the 'Miracle on the Hudson' possible.

The Golden Triangle

Hutterite Colonies are replacing the family farms of Montana. The cause of the financial collapse of the family farm is clear; the way to save it is far from obvious.

The Farm Program

Big agribusinesses have spent decades manipulating U.S. farm policy. One professor and his wife challenge the status quo hoping to improve the farm economy.

Visit the authors website:
https://www.amazon.com/T-H.
Harbinger/e/B00JEVD256

**Please connect and leave
messages with:**

T H. Harbinger

On Facebook

@harbinger_h

On Twitter

Made in the USA
Monee, IL
10 November 2021

81544546R00046